Popular Souvenir Plates

Monica Lynn Clements & Patricia Rosser Clements

WASCOTT, WIS.

Schiffer Publishing Ltd

4880 Lower Valley Rd. Atglen, PA 19310 USA

Dedication

For Jimmie O. Clements, Sr.

Designed by Bonnie M. Hensley
Layout by Randy L. Hensley
Typeset in Zapf Chancery BD BT/Times New Roman

ISBN: 0-7643-0535-2
Printed in China
1 2 3 4

Published by Schiffer Publishing Ltd.
4880 Lower Valley Road
Atglen, PA 19310
Phone: (610) 593-1777; Fax: (610) 593-2002
E-mail: Schifferbk@aol.com
Please write for a free catalog.
This book may be purchased from the publisher.
Please include $3.95 for shipping.

In Europe, Schiffer books are distributed by
Bushwood Books
6 Marksbury Avenue Kew Gardens
Surrey TW9 4JF England
Phone: 44 (0)181 392-8585;
Fax: 44 (0)181 392-9876
E-mail: Bushwd@aol.com

Please try your bookstore first.
We are interested in hearing from authors
with book ideas on related subjects.

Acknowledgements

Our thanks go to the many contributors who allowed us to
photograph the souvenir plates found in this book.

Contents

Introduction

Souvenir plates come in a variety of sizes and a myriad of designs. The only limit to the collector is how much money he or she wishes to invest. Design, size, and manufacturer are the criteria enthusiasts use when choosing these items. Found at tag sales and antiques shops, souvenir ware offers a bit of history and a glimpse into what tourists of the past have taken home from their travels.

This book covers the spectrum of souvenir plates made in North America and in foreign countries. While a concentration comes from Homer Laughlin plates and Vernon Kilns' varied designs, other American pottery companies are represented. Examples of Japanese imported plates as well as the English imports of Staffordshire and Wedgwood appear. The final chapter on "Foreign Plates" also includes souvenir plates marked "West Germany," "Made in Germany," "Made in Bavaria," and others.

The purpose of this book is not to set firm prices but to act as a guide. The prices of the souvenir plates reflect the combined experience of both authors in collecting and dealing in antiques. The prices represent the range of values observed throughout the United States.

Chapter One
History

Nostalgia created the desire for souvenirs. Travelers wanted to have a remembrance of where they journeyed themselves, or they wished to take a souvenir item to a friend or a loved one. Pottery and china companies filled the void by creating mementos in the form of souvenir ware. The plates depicted churches, cities, buildings, monuments, parks, fraternal organizations, schools, universities, tourist attractions, historical scenes, or special events.

Souvenir plates date back to the 1870s. With the Industrial Revolution came changes in society through the population shift from the country to the cities. Travel became more accessible around the turn of the century, and souvenir plates soared in popularity.

American and foreign made souvenir dishes became common. Noted pottery manufacturers such as East Liverpool Pottery and Buffalo Pottery introduced simple yet distinctive souvenir ware. Staffordshire and Wedgwood imported souvenir plates that depicted historical scenes. Plate designs marked "Made in Bavaria" and "Made in Germany" appeared.

Pennsylvania plate, East Liverpool Pottery Co., Philadelphia, Liberty Bell, 7 inches, ca. 1900–1903. $25-35.

New York plate, Buffalo Pottery, Niagara Falls plate, 7.5 inches, 1905. $15-20 as is.

Liverpool Pottery mark.

Buffalo Pottery mark.

District of Columbia plate, Wedgwood, Washington Monument, ca. 1920s. *Courtesy River City Mercantile Cos., Jefferson, Texas.* $50-60.

Massachusetts plate, Wedgwood, Faneuil Hall, 10.5 inches, 1930. *Courtesy River City Mercantile Cos.* $40-50.

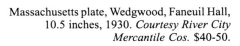

Scotland plate, Made in Germany, International Exhibition, Glasgow 1888, 9.5 inches. *Courtesy River City Mercantile Cos.* $45-55.

New York plate, Bavaria, Made in Germany, General View of Niagara Falls, ca. 1890s. *Courtesy of Shirley Falardeau.* $35-45.

New York plate, Made in West Germany, Niagara Falls, 10 inches, ca. 1930s. *Courtesy of Out 'n' Back Antiques, Bismarck, Arkansas.* $35-45.

Iowa plate, Made in Germany, High School, Waverly, Iowa, 5.75 inches, ca. 1920s. $18-28.

Around the turn of the century, civic groups, churches, fraternal organizations, and others wanted to celebrate the passing of important events with keepsakes. Commemorative plates served this purpose. Often, the plates were gifts to members. Souvenir plates with commemorative designs provided remembrances for centennials, sesquicentennials, or other notable events in cities, towns, or at churches.

Pennsylvania plate, Homer Laughlin, Eggshell, Georgian, decorated by World Wide Art Studio, Royal Arch Chapter 150th Anniversary plate, Lancaster, Pa. 1809-1959, 9.75 inches. $35-45.

Pennsylvania plate, Wright, Tyndale, & Van Roden, Grand Lodge of Pennsylvania, F. & A. M. Sesquicentennial, 9.25 inches, 1902. $95-125.

Kansas plate, Centennial of the State of Kansas, 8 inches, 1961. *Courtesy of Gertrude Templeton Sasser and Otis C. Sasser.* $10-12.

Pennsylvania plate, Kettlesprings Kilns, Somerset, Penna. Sesqui-Centennial, March 5 to July 5, 1954, 1804-1954, 10 inches. $12-18.

Decorated by World Wide Art Studios, 50th Anniversary Epworth United Methodist Church 1929-1979 plate, 10 inches, ca. 1979. *Courtesy of Margie Manning.* $8-12.

Tupperware Jubilee plate, 9.5 inches, 1957. *Courtesy of Out 'n' Back Antiques.* $12-18.

Although companies continued to provide souvenir plates, demand waned in the 1920s. With the construction of better roads and increasing ease of travel, souvenir plates came back into vogue by the 1930s. During the 1940s and 1950s, numerous pottery companies produced or designed souvenir plates.

Oriental imports appeared in the 1940s. Souvenir items with the mark of "Occupied Japan" bear evidence to this fact. Lefton imported items from Japan including quality souvenir ware treasured by collectors around the world.

Texas dish, Occupied Japan, 3 inches, ca. 1940s. *Courtesy of Cindy Porter.* $10-15.

Along with quality souvenir ware, other plates of lesser quality made their way into the market. By the 1950s, Japanese designs depicting American subjects took a place along side plates manufactured in the United States. American companies commissioned Japanese firms to produce souvenir ware.

Oriental companies used the Homer Laughlin designs as models. The plates from the Japanese counterparts had similar border designs. Upon close examination, the quality of the pottery, the color, and the design could not compare to the Homer Laughlin plates. The plates had no stamped mark on the back but sometimes had a sticker denoting the origin. Still, these items proved popular among souvenir plate enthusiasts.

English Potters

Throughout this century, commemorative and historical souvenir plates have been imported from England by gift shops or companies in the United States. The historical scenes and rich colors of the dishes make them popular as collector and decorative items. Noted names familiar to collectors are Adams; Rowland and Marsellus; and the John Roth Company.

The John Roth Company of Peoria, Illinois, imported Adams ware from 1920 to 1965. Adams goes back to the seventeenth century as a maker of fine pottery. Through its souvenir ware, the company has provided dishes with transfer designs. The mark of the John Roth Company, known as "Jonroth," can be found on plates along with the Old English Staffordshire mark. The plates depict historical scenes and other subjects common to souvenir ware. While the most common colors chosen for this pottery were blue and white, designs can be found in other colors.

Tennessee dish, Lefton with stamped mark in gold and sticker with mark, 5 inches, ca. 1950s. *Courtesy of Mary G. Moon.* $15-25.

Tennessee plate, Olde English Staffordshire Ware, The Hermitage, Home of Andrew Jackson, Olde English Staffordshire Ware, 10 inches, ca. 1950s. *Courtesy of Eric B. Cain.* $65-85.

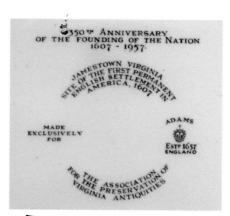

Old Church Tower plate marks.

Virginia plate, Adams, Olde English Staffordshire Ware, The Old Church Tower, Jamestown, 350th Anniversary of the Founding of the Nation 1607-1957, 10.5 inches. *Courtesy of Memory Lane Mall, Atlanta, Texas*. $65-85.

Kentucky plate, Olde English Staffordshire Ware, Jonroth, Old Fort Harrod Pioneer Memorial State Park, 6.75 inches, ca. 1960s. *Courtesy of Memory Lane Mall*. $45-55.

Massachusetts plate, Old English Staffordshire Ware, Souvenir of Salem, Mass., Adams, 8 inches, 1964. *Courtesy of Sarah Newton, Sarah's Antiques & Collectibles*. $55-65.

Massachusetts plate, Old English Staffordshire Ware, Jonroth, Bearskin Neck, Rockport, Mass., 7 inches, ca. 1950s. $45-55.

From the 1890s and into the 1930s, the New York firm of Rowland and Marsellus enlisted companies in England to manufacture souvenir ware to be sold in the United States. These imported dishes with transfer designs proved popular as evidenced by the large number of souvenir plates available. A notable trait of the Rowland and Marsellus plates is the rolled border.

Tennessee plate, Adams, Olde English Staffordshire Ware, Capitol of Tennessee, 10 inches, ca. 1950s. *Courtesy of Eric B. Cain.* $65-85.

Missouri plate, Rowland and Marsellus, Views of Springfield, Mo., 9 inches, 1913. *Courtesy of River City Mercantile Cos.* $145-155.

Ohio plate, Rowland and Marsellus, Views of Cincinnati, O, 9 inches, ca. 1920s. *Courtesy of River City Mercantile Cos.* $75-95.

Molly Pitcher at Battle of Monmouth, Rowland and Marsellus, 10 inches, ca. 1920s. *Courtesy of River City Mercantile Cos.* $75-85.

Noted Manufacturers and Decorators of Souvenir Plates

Clarice Cliff (1928–1964)

Seldom is souvenir ware associated with Clarice Cliff. The company manufactured Art Deco pottery between 1928 and 1935. In the late 1940s and into the 1950s, Clarice Cliff provided a type of ware with transfer designs. The plates in the souvenir ware are colorful and have become collectible.

Canadian plate, Clarice Cliff, Royal Canadian Mounted Police, 10.75 inches, ca. 1950s. *Courtesy of Melba Long.* $55-75.

Conrad Crafters, Inc. (1952)

The company began in 1952 and worked to design dinnerware. Since 1957, this company has decorated souvenir ware and gift items.

Maryland plate, signed Conrad Crafters, Cumberland, Maryland, 8 inches, ca. 1970s. *Courtesy of Gertrude Templeton Sasser and Otis C. Sasser.* $8-12.

Harker Pottery (1890–1972)

An Englishman, Benjamin Harker, bought a farm in Ohio where he began a small pottery operation in 1840. This was the beginning of what would become Harker Pottery. The coming years would bring a change in managers with the death of Harker. His two sons, Benjamin, Jr. and George, took over, but the Civil War caused changes in the company. Harker Pottery stayed in the family, and George's sons guided the company to the success it found as a producer of dinnerware until 1972, when the company went out of business.

Alabama plate, Harker China Company, Laureltron pattern, 9.5 inches, ca. 1950s. *Courtesy of Gertrude Templeton Sasser and Otis C. Sasser.* $12-18.

Kettlesprings Kilns, Alliance, Ohio (1950)

Founded in 1950, Kettlesprings Kilns designs and decorates commemorative plates.

Tennessee plate, Kettlesprings Kilns, Diamond Jubilee, Harriman, 10 inches, 1965. *Courtesy of Mary G. Moon.* $12-18.

Ohio plate, Kettlesprings Kilns, Wooster Sesquicentennial 1808-1958, 9.5 inches. $12-18.

Kettlesprings Kilns mark.

Edwin M. Knowles China Company (1900–1963)

The Knowles family had a strong reputation for manufacturing dinnerware. The company of Knowles, Taylor, Knowles paved the way, but Edwin Knowles formed his own company in 1900. The site of the first plant was Chester, West Virginia, and the company later moved to Newell, West Virginia.

Colorado plate, Edwin M. Knowles China, Garden of the Gods, 7 inches, ca. 1950s. *Courtesy of Old Mill Antiques.* $8-12.

Homer Laughlin Company (1871–present)

Homer Laughlin started a small pottery with his brother, Shakespeare, in East Liverpool, Ohio, in 1871. Their perseverance led them to achieve the art of making china. After he bought out his brother's interest in the company and became successful, Homer Laughlin sold his company.

By the early 1900s, the company flourished under the new management of Louis I. Aaron and his sons, Marcus and Charles. While Louis Aaron assumed the business side of the company, W.E. Wells, who acted as General Manager, headed the actual running of the company. Under this new management, the Homer Laughlin Company began to produce a vast amount of china. In 1905, the company built a pottery in Newell, West Virginia.

A popular pattern in tableware and in souvenir plates was Eggshell. Introduced in 1937, the variety of shapes included Eggshell Nautilus and Eggshell Georgian. Swing appeared in 1938. The Theme design honored the World's Fair of 1939. Homer Laughlin produced a large number of Eggshell plates. Later designs came in the 1940s with Cavalier, Jubilee, and Rhythm. During the post war years, the company became the largest manufacturer of pottery in the world.

In the late 1950s, Homer Laughlin decided to move into the area of producing hotel and restaurant china. This enduring company continues to produce quality china.

Kansas plate, Homer Laughlin, Eggshell, Cavalier, The Sunflower State, 9 inches, ca. 1950s. *Courtesy of Out 'n' Back Antiques.* $12-18.

Homer Laughlin mark.

California plate, Homer Laughlin, Eggshell, Cavalier, 7.75 x 7.75 inches ca. 1940s. *Courtesy of Mary G. Moon.* $12-18.

Ohio plate, Homer Laughlin Debutante, 1950. *Courtesy of Out 'n' Back Antiques.* $12-18.

Homer Laughlin mark.

Homer Laughlin Nautilus mark.

Alabama plate, Homer Laughlin Nautilus, The Cotton State, 10.25 inches, ca. 1940s. *Courtesy of Out 'n' Back Antiques.* $15-20.

Tennessee plate, Homer Laughlin, Eggshell, Theme, Carter House on Battlefield, Franklin, Tennessee, ca. 1940s. *Courtesy of Mary G. Moon.* $15-20.

Lefton China Company (1940–present)

Since 1940, Lefton has imported quality giftware and dishes made in Japan.

Mayer China Company (1881)

Joseph Mayer, an English potter, came to New York from England to begin a pottery business. The company has manufactured hotel and dinnerware along with souvenir items.

Pennsylvania plate, Mayer China, Borough of New Brighton, Pennsylvania, Inc. 1838, 1938-1963, 10 inches. $10-12.

Pennsylvania plate, Homer Laughlin, Rhythm, Pennsylvania The Keystone State, 10.5 inches, ca. 1940s. $8-12.

Sabin Industries, Inc. (1946–1979)

Samuel Sabin created his company to decorate china and glass. This company was in operation from 1946 until 1979 when a fire destroyed the plant. Sabin Industries then became part of Mt. Clemens Pottery in Mt. Clemens, Michigan.

A distinguishing characteristic was the Crest-O-Gold trim. Salem China made a majority of the plates decorated by Sabin. Other souvenir plates such as those from Taylor, Smith, and Taylor had the distinctive gold trim.

Salem China Company (1898)

Three disgruntled workers from Standard Pottery started Salem China Company in 1898, though it wasn't until 1918 that the company began to thrive. Under the direction of Floyd McKee, Salem China Company built a reputation for producing high quality dinnerware. Souvenir plates have been found with the Salem mark and the design of the Sabin Company with the Crest-O-Gold trim.

Arkansas plate, signed Sabin Crest-O-Gold, 10.5 inches, ca. 1950s. *Courtesy of Jackie McDonald.* $10-15.

Kansas plate, marked Salem and Sabin, Kansas, The Sunflower State, 10 inches, ca. 1960s. *Courtesy of Mary G. Moon.* $12-18.

Sanders Manufacturing Company (1918)

From 1918 through the 1950s, Sanders Manufacturing Company worked to decorate plates. The company concentrated on advertising and special orders until the 1950s, when it moved into the area of souvenir plate design. Several companies including Limoges provided plates for the designs.

Steubenville Pottery (1879-1959)

Steubenville Pottery built a reputation for manufacturing dinner sets. The company also designed and manufactured souvenir items for various gift shops.

Oklahoma plate, Sanders Manufacturing Company, 7.25 inches, ca. 1960s. $8-12.

Virginia plate, Mount Vernon, Steubenville, 10 inches, ca. 1960s. *Courtesy of JoAnn Askew.* $15-25.

Syracuse China Company (1841)

The operation of Syracuse China Company began in 1841 although under a different name. The company was known as Empire Pottery from 1855 until 1871. Up to that point, the company manufactured items from available clay such as bowls, crocks, and jugs. Empire Pottery introduced a line of white ware in the 1870s. The company name became Onondaga Pottery Company. In the 1960s, the company wanted to promote its line of Syracuse China and changed the company name to Syracuse China Company.

Syracuse China continued to manufacture dinnerware and fine china for the consumer. The company discontinued these lines in 1971 to devote production to ware for airlines, hotels, and restaurants.

Taylor, Smith, and Taylor (1899–1982)

This company was in operation from 1899 to 1982. The founders of the company were C. A. Smith and Colonel John N. Taylor. W. L. Smith and his son acquired the company in 1903. While Taylor, Smith, and Taylor produced exceptional dinnerware and kitchenware, souvenir plates have been found that bear the company's mark and Sabin's Crest-O-Gold trim.

Nebraska plate, Taylor, Smith, and Taylor, Nebraska City Centennial 1854-1954, 9 inches. *Courtesy of Out 'n' Back Antiques*. $12-18.

Missouri Pacific Lines plate, Syracuse China Company, Eagle Train Line plate, 10 inches, ca. 1960s. *Courtesy of Gold Leaf Antique Mall.* $350-375.

Syracuse China Co. mark.

Vernon Kilns (1916–1958)

Known first as Poxon China Company and then as Vernon Potteries, Vernon Kilns built a reputation for manufacturing souvenir ware. Rockwell Kent was the first of many artists to create distinctive designs. The earliest picture plate debuted in 1936 with the "Arkansaw Traveler." The first series that showcased Kent's talent was the "Our America" ware.

Arkansas plate, Vernon Kilns, The Arkansaw Traveler, 1936. *Courtesy of Out 'n' Back Antiques.* $65-75.

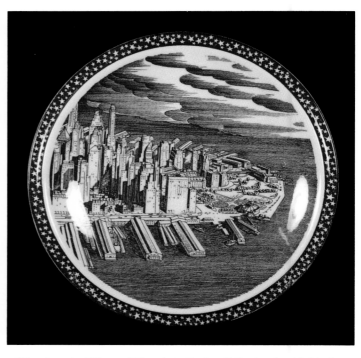

"Our America" Vernon Kilns plate, Rockwell Kent, artist, 10.5 inches, ca. 1930s. *Courtesy of Out 'n' Back Antiques.* $95-125.

Vernon Kilns produced commemorative and souvenir ware until 1958. Along with manufacturing ashtrays, spoon holders, and other souvenir items, the company produced commemorative plates through special order for private companies and organizations. Vernon Kilns offered series of plates such as "Bits of the Middle West" and "Bits of the South." Souvenir plates also depicted cities, monuments, state maps, parks, hospitals, historical figures, organizations, schools, and universities.

California ashtray, Vernon Kilns, 5 inches, ca. 1940s. *Courtesy of Out 'n' Back Antiques.* $15-25.

Wisconsin plate, Vernon Kilns, 50th Anniversary of A.H. Bluemke & Sons Co., Rosendale, Wis., 1903-1953, 10.5 inches. *Courtesy of Out 'n' Back Antiques*. $25-35.

Woodman Insurance Company plate, Vernon Kilns, 10.5 inches, ca. 1940s. *Courtesy of Out 'n' Back Antiques*. $25-35.

One of four plates from Bits of the Middle West series, Vernon Kilns, 8.5 inches, ca. 1940s. *Courtesy of Out 'n' Back Antiques*. $55-65.

Cypress Swamp plate, one of four plates from Bits of the Old South series, Vernon Kilns, 8.5 inches, ca. 1940s. *Courtesy of Out 'n' Back Antiques.* $45-55.

A Southern Mansion plate, from Bits of the Old South series, Vernon Kilns, 8.5 inches, ca. 1940s. *Courtesy of Out 'n' Back Antiques.* $45-55.

Down on the Levee, from the Bits of the Old South series, Vernon Kilns, 8.5 inches, ca. 1940s. *Courtesy of Out 'n' Back Antiques.* $45-55.

South Carolina plate, Vernon Kilns, Greenville, South Carolina, 10.5 inches, ca. 1940s. *Courtesy of Out 'n' Back Antiques.* $25-35.

Texas plate, Vernon Kilns, 10.5 inches, ca. 1940s. *Courtesy of Out 'n' Back Antiques.* $25-35.

The common size of the picture plates was 10.5 inches. The colors of the drawings were blue, brown, or maroon on a cream colored background. In addition to the Vernon Kilns mark, the back of the plates often contained a paragraph that explained the historical significance of the plate design or a state seal.

Denver, Vernon Kilns, Colorado plate, 10.5 inches, ca. 1940s. *Courtesy of Out 'n' Back Antiques*. $25-35.

Vernon Kilns mark.

Louisiana plate, Vernon Kilns, St. Francisville, West Felliciana, Grace Episcopal Church, 10.5 inches, ca. 1950s. *Courtesy of Out 'n' Back Antiques*. $25-35.

Grace Episcopal Church plate historical information and mark.

GRACE EPISCOPAL CHURCH
St. Francisville, Louisiana

Grace Church was organized in 1828 with the Rev. William R. Bowman as its first Rector. The present edifice was erected in 1858 while the Rev. Daniel S. Lewis was Rector. Bishop Leonidas Polk, later, General C.S.A. laid the cornerstone. The Church was struck by Union shell-fire during the Civil War, and some of these scars are still evident. It is the second oldest Episcopal Church in Louisiana. The present Rector is the Rev. Robert G. Donaldson.

VERNON KILNS
U.S.A.

World Wide Art Studios, Covington, Tennessee

This company decorates commemorative and souvenir plates. The World Wide Art Studios mark appears on Homer Laughlin plates in the Eggshell pattern. This company has built a reputation for decorating plates depicting churches.

Karnack Methodist Church, decorated by Worldwide Art Studios, 10 inches, ca. 1950s. *Courtesy of Bill Williams.* $8-12.

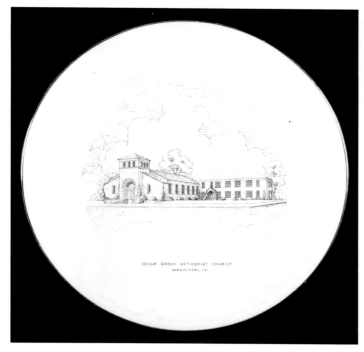

Cedar Grove Methodist Church plate, Shreveport, Louisiana, Homer Laughlin theme plate decorated by World Wide Art Studios, ca. 1940s. *Courtesy of Memory Lane Mall.* $8-12.

Homer Laughlin Theme mark and the World Wide Art Studios mark.

Chapter Two

Souvenir Plates of the United States

Alabama

Alabama plate, Design Patented, 6 inches, ca. 1960s. $7-12.

Alabama plate, Homer Laughlin, 9 inches, ca. 1950s. $12-18.

Alabama plate, Homer Laughlin, 10 inches, ca. 1950s. *Courtesy of Old Mill Antiques.* $15-25.

Alaska

Alabama plate, Homer Laughlin design, ca. 1950s. *Courtesy of Mr. and Mrs. Earl Cox.* $7-11.

Alaska plate, Godfred & Associates, 10 inches, ca. 1950s. $14-18.

Alabama plate, Vernon Kilns, Huntsville, Alabama, 10.5 inches, ca. 1940s. *Courtesy of Out 'n' Back Antiques.* $25-35.

Alaska plate, Made in Japan, 8.5 inches, ca. 1960s. *Courtesy of Gertrude Templeton Sasser and Otis C. Sasser.* $7-11.

Arizona

Alaska, The 49th State plate, 7 inches, ca. 1950s. $6-12.

Arizona, Made in Korea, The Grand Canyon State stoneware plate, 10.5 inches, ca. 1960s. $5-10.

Alaska plate, Vernon Kilns, picture map plate of Alaska, 10.5 inches, ca. 1940s. *Courtesy of Out 'n' Back Antiques.* $35-45.

Arizona plate, 10.25 inches, ca. 1950s. $6-10.

Arizona, Grand Canyon National Park, 7 inches, ca. 1960s. *Courtesy of Gertrude Templeton Sasser and Otis C. Sasser.* $6-10.

Arizona plate, 7 inches, ca. 1960s. *Courtesy of Old Mill Antiques.* $8-12.

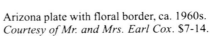

Arizona plate with floral border, ca. 1960s. *Courtesy of Mr. and Mrs. Earl Cox.* $7-14.

Arizona plate, Sabin Crest-O-Gold, 7.25 inches, ca. 1950s. $8-12.

Arizona plate, Johnson Brothers, Made in England, The Grand Canyon, The Arizona Plate, 10.75 inches, ca. 1950s. $35-55.

Arizona plate, The Grand Canyon State, 7 inches, ca. 1950s. $5-8.

Arizona plate, 8 inches, ca. 1950s. *Courtesy of Out 'n' Back Antiques.* $5-10.

Arkansas

Arizona plate, Vernon Kilns, 10.5 inches, ca. 1950s. *Courtesy of Out 'n' Back Antiques.* $25-35.

Arkansas plate, Vacationland, 10 inches, ca. 1950s. *Courtesy of Mary G. Moon.* $10-15.

Arizona plate, Vernon Kilns, Gateway to the Grand Canyon, Williams, Arizona plate, ca. 1940s. *Courtesy of Out 'n' Back Antiques.* $25-35.

Arkansas plate, Mountain Village 1890, Bull Shoals, 9.25 inches, ca. 1960s. $8-12.

Arkansas plate, measures 10 inches, 1953. *Courtesy of Louise Martin.* $8-12.

Arkansas plate with gold border, 6.25 inches, ca. 1960s. $12-18.

Arkansas plate, Christ of the Ozarks, Eureka Springs, 9 inches, ca. 1960s. $9-15.

Arkansas plate, ca. 1960s. $12-18.

Arkansas plate, Hot Springs National Park, 8 inches, ca. 1960s.
Courtesy of Gertrude Templeton Sasser and Otis C. Sasser. $7-12.

Arkansas plate, Homer Laughlin, Best China, Hot Springs, 9.75 inches,
ca. 1960s. $12-18.

Arkansas plate, 10 inches, ca. 1950s. $6-12.

Arkansas plate, Greetings from Arkansas, 8 inches, ca. 1960s. $4-8.

Arkansas, Texarkana Arkansas, and Texas Centennial plate, 10 inches, 1973. *Courtesy of Mary G. Moon.* $5-10.

Arkansas commemorative plate, Vernon Kilns, ca. 1943.
Courtesy of Gold Leaf Antique Mall. $15-25 as is.

Arkansas plate, Crater of Diamonds, Murfreesboro, 7 inches, ca. 1960s. *Courtesy of Gertrude Templeton Sasser and Otis C. Sasser.* $4-8.

Arkansas plate, Victorian Homes, Eureka Springs, 6.5 inches, ca. 1950s. *Courtesy of Gertrude Templeton Sasser and Otis C. Sasser.* $8-12.

Arkansas plate, Made in Japan, 6 inches, ca. 1960s. $4-8.

Arkansas plate with green and gold border, 10.25 inches, ca. 1960s. *Courtesy of Jackie McDonald.* $12-18.

Arkansas plate, Hope, Arkansas Centennial, Cairo & Fulton Railroad, 7.25 inches, 1975. $15-20.

Arkansas plate with gold border, 8 inches, ca. 1960s. *Courtesy of Mr. and Mrs. Earl Cox.* $4-8.

Arkansas, Land of Opportunity plate, ca. 1960s. *Courtesy of Mr. and Mrs. Earl Cox.* $4-8.

Arkansas plate, Vernon Kilns, 10.5 inches, ca. 1940s. *Courtesy of Out 'n' Back Antiques.* $25-35.

California

California plate, Los Angeles, 9 inches, ca. 1940s. *Courtesy of Mary G. Moon.* $12-18.

California plate, Made in Japan, Knotts Berry Farm and Ghost Town, 6 inches, ca. 1960s. *Courtesy of Mary G. Moon.* $4-8.

California plate, Made in Japan, San Francisco, 10 inches, ca. 1950s. *Courtesy of Mary G. Moon.* $5-10.

California plate, Made in Japan, 10.5 inches, ca. 1970s. $6-12.

California plate, THRIFCO, Made in Japan, California Missions, 4 inches, ca. 1960s. $4-8.

California plate, 8.25 inches, ca. 1960s. $8-12.

California plate, paper sticker with Made in Japan, A Quality Product, Knotts Berry Farm, Buena Park, 8.5 inches, ca. 1960s. *Courtesy of Gertrude Templeton Sasser and Otis C. Sasser.* $6-12.

California plate, 7.25 inches, ca. 1960s.
Courtesy of Mr. and Mrs. Earl Cox. $8-12.

California plate, 9 inches, ca. 1950s. *Courtesy of Gertrude Templeton Sasser and Otis C. Sasser.* $12-18.

California plate, Redwoods, 9 inches, ca. 1960s. $8-12.

California plate, Vernon Kilns, Colorful San Francisco, 10.5 inches, ca. 1950s. *Courtesy of Out 'n' Back Antiques.* $25-35.

California plate, Long Beach Grand Opera Premiere Performance, 9.5 inches, March 28, 1979. *Courtesy of Out 'n' Back Antiques.* $12-15.

Californina plate, Vernon Kilns, Mission San Rafael Arcangel, designed by Eugenia Brady, 8.5 inches, ca. 1940s. *Courtesy of Out 'n' Back Antiques.* $45-55.

Colorado

Colorado plate with green border, 7 inches, ca. 1950s. *Courtesy of Mary G. Moon.* $12-18.

Colorado plate, Pikes Peak, 7 inches, ca. 1940s. *Courtesy of Mary G. Moon.* $5-10.

Colorado plate, paper sticker with Made in Japan, A Quality Product, Pikes Peak, 10 inches, ca. 1950s. $7-11.

Colorado heart shaped plate, Rush to the Rockies Centennial, 6 x 6 inches, 1959. *Courtesy of Mary G. Moon*. $7-11.

Colorado plate, Norcrest Fine China, hand painted, Colorado Columbine, 8.25 inches, ca. 1960s. *Courtesy of Mary G. Moon*. $5-10.

Colorado plate, Colorful Colorado, 8.25 inches, ca. 1960s. $5-10.

Colorado plate, by Vitette's Arts, Air Force Academy, Colorado Springs, 8.25 inches, ca. 1960s. $12-18.

Colorado plate, Colorful Colorado with gold border, 8 inches, ca. 1950s. *Courtesy of Gertrude Templeton Sasser and Otis C. Sasser.* $7-11.

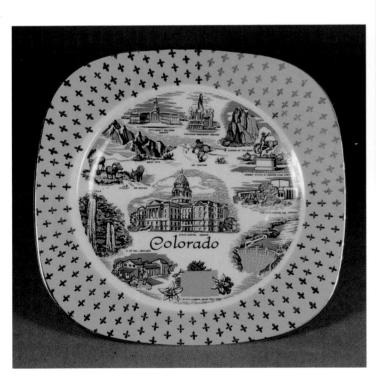

Colorado plate, Homer Laughlin, Eggshell, Cavalier, 7.75 x 7.75 inches, ca. 1940s. $16-22.

Colorado plate, Colorful Colorado, 10 inches, ca. 1960s. *Courtesy of Gertrude Templeton Sasser and Otis C. Sasser.* $10-15.

Colorado plate, Royal Gorge, 7 inches, ca. 1950s. *Courtesy of Old Mill Antiques.* $7-11.

Colorado plate, Homer Laughlin, Snow White, Top of the Nation, 9.25 inches, ca. 1950s. *Courtesy of Gold Leaf Antique Mall.* $15-22.

Colorado plate, North Pole, 7 inches, ca. 1950s. *Courtesy of Out 'n' Back Antiques.* $4-8.

Colorado plate, Vernon Kilns, Colorado Springs, 10.5 inches, ca. 1950s. *Courtesy of Out 'n' Back Antiques.* $25-35.

Colorado plate, Vernon Kilns, Colorado Springs, 10.5 inches, ca. 1950s. *Courtesy of Out 'n' Back Antiques.* $25-35.

Colorado plate, The Broadmoor, Colorado Springs, ca. 1950s. *Courtesy of Out 'n' Back Antiques.* $8-12.

Colorado plate, Vernon Kilns, Denver, 10.5 inches, ca. 1950s. *Courtesy of Out 'n' Back Antiques.* $25-35.

Connecticut

Connecticut plate, Nutmeg State, 9.5 inches, ca. 1950s. *Courtesy of Gertrude Templeton Sasser and Otis C. Sasser.* $12-18.

Connecticut plate, 9.25 inches, ca. 1950s. *Courtesy of Mr. and Mrs. Earl Cox.* $8-12.

Connecticut plate, Kettlesprings Kilns, 10.25 inches, ca. 1950s. *Courtesy of Mary G. Moon.* $18-25.

Connecticut plate, 9.25 inches, ca. 1950s. $8-12.

Delaware

Delaware plate, 9.25 inches, ca. 1960s. *Courtesy of Mr. and Mrs. Earl Cox.* $8-12.

Delaware plate, The Blue Hen State, 8.5 inches x 8.5 inches, ca. 1960s. *Courtesy of Out 'n' Back Antiques.* $4-8.

District of Columbia

District of Columbia plate, Capitol Souvenir Co., The Capitol, Washington, D.C., 7 inches, ca. 1960s. $12-18.

District of Columbia plate, signed Design Patented, Washington, D.C., 7.5 inches, ca. 1950s. *Courtesy of Gertrude Templeton Sasser and Otis C. Sasser.* $4-8.

District of Columbia plate, The Capitol, Washington, D.C., 7.75 inches, ca. 1960s. *Courtesy of Old Mill Antiques.* $12-18.

District of Columbia plate, Washington, 8 inches, ca. 1960s. *Courtesy of Gertrude Templeton Sasser and Otis C. Sasser.* $12-18.

District of Columbia plate, Vernon Kilns, Liberty with George Washington, 10.5 inches, ca. 1950s. *Courtesy of Memory Lane Mall.* $25-35.

District of Columbia plate, Syracuse China Company, The Capitol, Washington, D. C., 5.5 inches, ca. 1940s. *Courtesy of Old Mill Antiques.* $15-20.

District of Columbia plate, Syracuse China Company, Mt. Vernon, Washington, D. C., 5.5 inches, ca. 1940s. *Courtesy of Old Mill Antiques.* $15-20.

District of Columbia plate, Syracuse China Company, depicts George and Martha Washington, Washington, D. C., 5.5 inches, ca. 1940s. *Courtesy of Old Mill Antiques.* $15-20.

Washington, D.C. plate, 8 inches, ca. 1950s. *Courtesy of Out 'n' Back Antiques.* $15-20.

Florida

Florida plate, Vernon Kilns, Picture Map of Florida, The Sunshine State, 10 inches, ca. 1950s. *Courtesy of Mary G. Moon.* $25-35.

Florida plate, 8 inches, ca. 1960s. $5-10.

Florida plate, 8 inches, ca. 1960s. *Courtesy of Mary G. Moon.* $5-10.

Florida plate, 10.5 inches, ca. 1960s. $8-12.

Florida plate, Kenmar, Japan, 10.5 inches, ca. 1960s. $7-12.

Florida plate, Life is a Beach, Hollywood, Fl., 9 inches, ca. 1970s. *Courtesy of Gertrude Templeton Sasser and Otis C. Sasser.* $4-8.

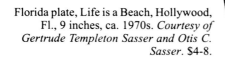

Florida plate, 10 inches, ca. 1950s. *Courtesy of Old Mill Antiques.* $4-8.

Florida plate, signed Walt Disney Productions, Japan, Walt Disney World, 7.5 inches, ca. 1980s. $8-12.

Florida plate, 8.75 inches, ca. 1960s. *Courtesy of JoAnn Askew.* $10-15.

Florida plate, 10.5 inches, ca. 1960s. *Courtesy of Old Mill Antiques.* $12-18.

Florida plate, The Sunshine State, 10 inches, ca. 1950s. *Courtesy of Mr. and Mrs. Earl Cox*. $4-8.

Florida plate, Vernon Kilns, Historic Saint Augustine, 10.5 inches, ca. 1950s. *Courtesy of Out 'n' Back Antiques*. $25-35.

Florida plate, Vernon Kilns, 10.5 inches, ca. 1950s. *Courtesy of Out 'n' Back Antiques*. $25-35.

Georgia

Georgia plate, Atlanta Georgia, 9 inches, ca. 1950s. *Courtesy of Mary G. Moon.* $4-8.

Georgia plate, The Empire State of the South, 10 inches, ca. 1960s. $8-12.

Georgia plate, 10 inches, ca. 1950s. $5-10.

Georgia plate, Stone Mountain, 9.5 inches, 1971. $10-15.

Georgia plate, The Empire State of the South, 9 inches, ca. 1950s. $12-18.

Georgia plate, 9.25 inches, ca. 1950s. *Courtesy of JoAnn Askew*. $8-12.

Georgia plate, 9 inches, ca. 1960s. *Courtesy of Mr. and Mrs. Earl Cox.* $8-12.

Georgia plate, Stone Mountain, has gold border, 9 inches, ca. 1960s. *Courtesy of JoAnn Askew*. $8-12.

Hawaii

Georgia plate, Vernon Kilns, Warm Springs, 10.5 inches, ca. 1950s. *Courtesy of Out 'n' Back Antiques*. $25-35.

Hawaii plate, Made in Japan, The Aloha State, 8 inches, ca. 1950s. $7-11.

Hawaii plate, The 50th State, Aloha, 10.25 inches, ca. 1960s. $7-11.

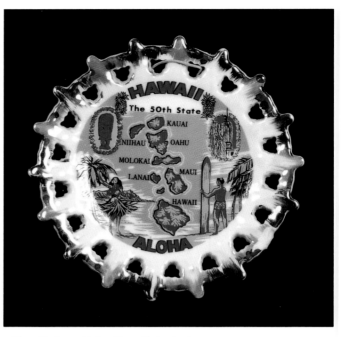

Hawaii plate, Hawaii The 50th State, Aloha plate, 9 inches, ca. 1950s. $8-12.

Hawaii plate, Aloha, Hawaii, 7.5 inches, ca. 1960s. *Courtesy of Gertrude Templeton Sasser and Otis C. Sasser.* $4-8.

Hawaii plate, Aloha, Hawaii, The 50th State, 9 inches, ca. 1960s. *Courtesy of Kenneth L. Surratt, Jr.* $8-12.

Idaho

Illinois

Idaho plate, The Gem State, 7 inches, ca. 1950s. *Courtesy of Gertrude Templeton Sasser and Otis C. Sasser.* $7-11.

Illinois plate, 10 inches, ca. 1960s. $9-14.

Illinois plate, Chicago, The City Beautiful, 8 inches, ca. 1950s. $4-8.

Illinois plate, with map, 7 inches, ca. 1950s. *Courtesy of Kenneth L. Surratt, Jr.* $4-8.

Illinois plate, Land O' Lincoln, ca. 1950s. *Courtesy of Mr. and Mrs. Earl Cox.* $4-8.

Illinois plate, 9.25 inches, ca. 1960s. *Courtesy of JoAnn Askew.* $8-12.

Illinois plate, Vernon Kilns, Chicago, 10.5 inches, ca. 1950s. *Courtesy of Out 'n' Back Antiques.* $25-35.

Indiana

Indiana plate, The Hoosier State, Homer Laughlin, 9 inches, ca. 1950s. *Courtesy of Kenneth L. Surratt, Jr.* $8-12.

Indiana plate, Kettlesprings Kilns, The Hoosier State, 10.25 inches, ca. 1960s. *Courtesy of Old Mill Antiques.* $18-22.

Indiana plate, Vernon Kilns, 10.5 inches, ca. 1950s. *Courtesy of Old Mill Antiques.* $25-35.

Indiana plate, Carlsbad BFHS China, Made in Austria, Muncie Indiana Courthouse, 8.5 inches, ca. 1930s. $18-30.

Iowa

Iowa plate, Homer Laughlin, 9.25 inches, ca. 1950s. *Courtesy of Mary G. Moon.* $8-12.

Iowa plate, 7 inches, ca. 1960s. *Courtesy of Mr. and Mrs. Earl Cox.* $4-8.

Iowa plate, Homer Laughlin, with red and gold border, ca. 1960s. *Courtesy of Gertrude Templeton Sasser and Otis C. Sasser.* $12-18.

Kansas

Kansas plate, 7 inches, ca. 1960s. *Courtesy of Mr. and Mrs. Earl Cox.* $4-8.

Kansas plate, Centennial of the State of Kansas 1861-1961, 9.25 inches. *Courtesy of Mary G. Moon.* $5-10.

Kansas plate, with buffalo, 10.25 inches, ca. 1980s. $5-10.

Kansas plate, Boot Hill, Dodge City, 10 inches, ca. 1980s. *Courtesy of Memory Lane Mall.* $15-20.

Kansas plate, Centennial of the State of Kansas, 1861-1961, signed Sabin. *Courtesy of Memory Lane Mall.* $12-18.

Kansas plate, American Ironstone,
Wichita Centennial 1870-1970,
10.25 inches. $18-22.

Kansas plate, signed Taylor, Smith, and Taylor, U. S. A.,
Wichita Terminal Elevators, Inc., Wichita, Kansas, 10 inches, ca.
1930s. $18-25.

Kansas plate, Homer Laughlin, and Art Studio, Loyal Order of Moose,
Wichita, Kansas, 9.5 inches, ca. 1960s. $15-20.

Kentucky

Kentucky plate, The Blue Grass State, 8 inches, ca. 1960s. $4-8.

Kentucky plate, 7.25 inches, ca. 1960s. $12-18.

Kentucky plate, Kentucky Dam-Kentucky Lake, 9.25 inches, ca. 1960s. $12-18.

Kentucky plate, signed Preston-Hopkinson, 10 inches, ca. 1970s. $12-18.

Kentucky plate, 10 inches, ca. 1970s. *Courtesy of Gertrude Templeton Sasser and Otis C. Sasser.* $8-12.

Kentucky plate, signed Dixie, Japan, The Blue Grass State, 7.5 inches x 7.5 inches, ca. 1970s. $5-10.

Kentucky plate, Homer Laughlin Eggshell, Nautilus, 10 inches, ca. 1940s. *Courtesy of Old Mill Antiques.* $12-18.

Louisiana

Louisiana plate, Vernon Kilns, with scenes from State of Louisiana, U. S. A., 10 inches, ca. 1940s. $25-35.

Louisiana plate, Made in Japan, Courtyard in the French Quarter, New Orleans, La., 3.88 inches, ca. 1960s. *Courtesy of Mary G. Moon.* $5-8.

Louisiana plate, New Orleans, La., 8 inches, ca. 1960s. $5-10.

Louisiana plate, New Orleans, America's Most Interesting City, 9 inches, ca. 1980s. *Courtesy of Gertrude Templeton Sasser and Otis C. Sasser.* $15-20.

Louisiana plate, The Pelican State, 9.5 inches, ca. 1960s. *Courtesy of Gertrude Templeton Sasser and Otis C. Sasser.* $8-12.

Louisiana plate, The Creole State, with gold border, 9 inches, ca. 1960s. *Courtesy of Jennie's Antique Mall.* $18-20.

Louisiana plate, The Creole State, with green and gold border, 9.5 inches, ca. 1960s. *Courtesy of Gertrude Templeton Sasser and Otis C. Sasser.* $10-15.

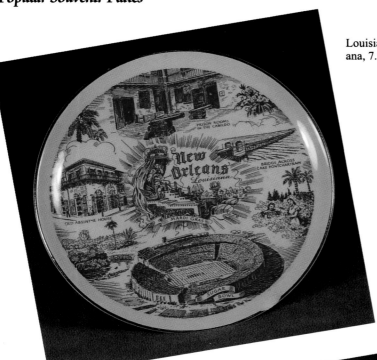

Louisiana plate, New Orleans, Louisiana, 7.25 inches, ca. 1950s. $10-15.

Louisiana plate, The Pelican State, 9.25 inches, ca. 1950s. *Courtesy of JoAnn Askew.* $12-18.

Louisiana plate, New Orleans, 9.5 inches, ca. 1980s. *Courtesy of Old Mill Antiques.* $15-20.

Louisiana plate, New Orleans, La., 10.75 inches, ca. 1960s. *Courtesy of JoAnn Askew.* $12-18.

Louisiana plate, Vernon Kilns, St. Martinsville, La. St. Martins Catholic Church, 10.5 inches, ca. 1950s. *Courtesy of Out 'n' Back Antiques.* $25-35.

Louisiana plate, The Pelican State, 9.25 inches, ca. 1950s. *Courtesy of Mr. and Mrs. Earl Cox.* $8-12.

Maine

Maine plate, The Pine Tree State, 9 inches, ca. 1950s. $10-15.

Maine plate, 9 inches, ca. 1960s. *Courtesy of Out 'n' Back Antiques.* $10-15.

Maine plate, 9 inches, ca. 1950s. *Courtesy of Out 'n' Back Antiques.* $10-15.

Maryland

Maryland plate, Maryland, America in Miniature, 9 inches, ca. 1950s. $4-8.

Maryland plate, Adam Antique by Steubenville, Sotterley 1730, Saint Mary's County, Maryland, 9.75 inches, ca. 1960s. $15-25.

Maryland plate, The Old Line State, 10 inches, ca. 1960s. *Courtesy of Out 'n' Back Antiques*. $5-10.

Maryland plate, Morgan Hopper China, 10 inches, ca. 1950s. *Courtesy of Out 'n' Back Antiques*. $10-15.

Massachusetts

Massachusetts plate, 7 inches, ca. 1970s. *Courtesy of Mr. and Mrs. Earl Cox.* $8-12

Massachusetts plate, Homer Laughlin, decorated by Worldwide Art Studio, Paul Revere's House, Boston, Mass., ca. 1960s. *Courtesy of Mary G. Moon.* $15-20.

Massachusetts plate, Cape Cod, Massachusetts, 9.25 inches, ca. 1980s. $18-22.

Massachusetts plate, Historic Boston, 9 inches, ca. 1980s. $22-30.

Massachusetts plate, Vernon Kilns, Salem, 10.5 inches, ca. 1950s. *Courtesy of Out 'n' Back Antiques.* $25-35.

Massachusetts plate, 8 inches, ca. 1950s. *Courtesy of Out 'n' Back Antiques.* $10-15.

Massachusetts plate, Vernon Kilns, Boston, 10.5 inches, ca. 1950s. *Courtesy of Out 'n' Back Antiques.* $25-35.

Michigan

Michigan plate, Tahquamenon Falls, Newberry, Mich., 9 inches, ca. 1930s. $4-8.

Michigan plate, ca. 1950s. *Courtesy of Mr. and Mrs. Earl Cox.* $4-8.

Minnesota

Minnesota plate, signed Sabin, The Gopher State, 9 inches, ca. 1950s. $8-12.

Minnesota plate, Land of 10,000 Lakes, 8.5 inches, ca. 1980s. *Courtesy of Gertrude Templeton Sasser and Otis C. Sasser.* $5-10.

Minnesota plate, 9.25 inches, ca. 1960s. *Courtesy of JoAnn Askew.* $4-8.

Minnesota plate, Vernon Kilns, 10.5 inches, ca. 1940s. *Courtesy of Out 'n' Back Antiques.* $25-35.

Minnesota plate, 9.25 inches, ca. 1960s. *Courtesy of Mr. and Mrs. Earl Cox.* $4-8.

Minnesota plate, Land of 10,000 Lakes, 9 inches, ca. 1950s. *Courtesy of Out 'n' Back Antiques.* $4-8.

Mississippi

Mississippi plate, with pink border, 10 inches, ca. 1960s. $5-10.

Mississippi plate, Sabin, Crest-O-Gold, 9 inches, ca. 1950s. $12-18.

Mississippi plate, 9.5 inches, ca. 1960s. *Courtesy of Gertrude Templeton Sasser and Otis C. Sasser*. $4-8.

Mississippi plate, 10.25 inches, ca. 1960s. $5-8.

Mississippi plate, 9 inches, ca. 1950s.
Courtesy of Jennie's Antique Mall. $8-12.

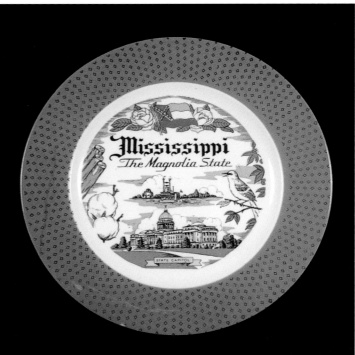

Mississippi plate, Homer Laughlin, Eggshell, Cavalier, The Magnolia
State, 10.25 inches, ca. 1940s. *Courtesy of Old Mill Antiques.* $18-22.

Mississippi plate, The Magnolia State, 10.25 inches, ca. 1980s.
Courtesy of Old Mill Antiques. $8-12.

Mississippi plate, 9.25 inches, ca. 1950s. *Courtesy of JoAnn Askew.* $5-10.

Mississippi plate, ca. 1950s. *Courtesy of Mr. and Mrs. Earl Cox.* $4-8.

Mississippi plate, The Magnolia State, 10 inches, ca. 1960s. *Courtesy of JoAnn Askew.* $12-18.

Missouri

Missouri plate, Lake of the Ozarks, Mo., ca. 1950s. *Courtesy of Mary G. Moon.* $8-12.

Missouri plate, 9 inches, ca. 1950s. $4-8.

Missouri plate, Excelsior Springs Mo., 7.25 inches, ca. 1960s. $8-12.

Missouri plate, 9.25 inches, ca. 1960s. $8-12.

Missouri plate, Homer Laughlin, Rhythm, 10 inches, ca. 1950s. $12-18.

Missouri plate, Old Matt's Cabin Missouri-Ozarks Memorial Museum, ca. 1950s. *Courtesy of Memory Lane Mall.* $8-12.

Missouri plate, signed Sabin, 8.5 inches, ca. 1950s. *Courtesy of Gertrude Templeton Sasser and Otis C. Sasser.* $12-18.

Missouri plate, Made in Japan, Missouri Gateway to the West, 6 inches, ca. 1960s. *Courtesy of Old Mill Antiques.* $5-10.

Missouri plate, Shepherd of the Hills Missouri, 6 inches, ca. 1960s. *Courtesy of Jackie McDonald*. $15-20.

Missouri plate, Independence, Mo., 10.5 inches, ca. 1950s. *Courtesy of Old Mill Antiques*. $22-30.

Missouri plate, 7.25 inches, ca. 1960s. *Courtesy of Mary G. Moon*. $4-8.

Missouri plate, 7 inches, ca. 1960s. *Courtesy of Mr. and Mrs. Earl Cox.* $6-12.

Missouri plate, Vernon Kilns, 10.5 inches, ca. 1940s. *Courtesy of Out 'n' Back Antiques.* $25-35.

Missouri plate, Vernon Kilns, Veiled Prophet, St. Louis Annual Parade & Ball since 1878, 10.5 inches, ca. 1940s. *Courtesy of Out 'n' Back Antiques.* $25-35.

Montana

Montana plate, signed Sabin Crest-O-Gold, The Treasure State, 6 inches, ca. 1950s. $10-15.

Montana plate, 7.5 inches, ca. 1970s. *Courtesy of Mr. and Mrs. Earl Cox.* $4-8.

Nebraska

Nebraska plate, The Beef State, 7 inches, ca. 1960s. *Courtesy of Mr. and Mrs. Earl Cox.* $4-8.

Nebraska plate, The Beef State, 9 inches, ca. 1950s. *Courtesy of Mary G. Moon.* $12-18.

Nebraska plate, The Cornhusker State, 7.5 inches, ca. 1980s. *Courtesy of Old Mill Antiques.* $8-12.

Nebraska plate, Vernon Kilns, Lincoln Nebraska's Capital "City of Beauty and Culture," 10.5 inches, ca. 1940s. *Courtesy of Out 'n' Back Antiques.* $25-35.

Nebraska plate, Pioneer Village, ca. 1950s. *Courtesy of Out 'n' Back Antiques.* $9-12.

Nebraska plate, Vernon Kilns, 10.5 inches, ca. 1940s. *Courtesy of Out 'n' Back Antiques.* $25-35.

Nevada

Nevada plate, Boulder Dam, Nevada, 6 inches, ca. 1960s. *Courtesy of Mary G. Moon.* $4-8.

Nevada plate, Nevada Centennial 1864-1964, 10 inches. $5-10.

Nevada plate, Hoover Dam, Nevada, 10 inches, ca. 1950s. *Courtesy of Louise Martin.* $6-12.

Nevada plate, Fabulous Las Vegas, 4 inches, ca. 1950s. *Courtesy of Gertrude Templeton Sasser and Otis C. Sasser.* $4-8.

Nevada plate, Las Vegas Nevada, 10.75 inches, ca. 1970s. *Courtesy of JoAnn Askew.* $8-12

Nevada plate, Homer Laughlin, Rhythm, Fremont St. at Night, Las Vegas, Nevada, 8 inches, ca. 1940s. *Courtesy of Jackie McDonald.* $12-18.

Nevada plate, Vernon Kilns, The Silver State, 10.5 inches, ca. 1940s. *Courtesy of Out 'n' Back Antiques.* $25-35.

Nevada plate, 9 inches, ca. 1960s. *Courtesy of Mr. and Mrs. Earl Cox.* $4-8.

Nevada plate, Vernon Kilns, Las Vegas, 10.5 inches, ca. 1940s. *Courtesy of Out 'n' Back Antiques.* $25-35.

New Hampshire

New Hampshire plate, The Granite State, 9 inches, ca. 1960s. *Courtesy of Mr. and Mrs. Earl Cox.* $4-8.

New Jersey

New Jersey, Homer Laughlin, 8 inches, ca. 1950s. *Courtesy of Out 'n' Back Antiques.* $15-25.

New Mexico

New Mexico plate, Fine Staffordshire Ware, Made in England, Carlsbad Caverns, decorated by ENCO, 10 inches, ca. 1960s. *Courtesy of Mary G. Moon.* $30-35.

New Mexico plate, Fine American Ironstone, by ENCO National, Carlsbad Caverns National Park, Made in U. S. A., 10 inches, ca. 1960s. $22-30.

New Mexico plate, Land of Enchantment, 9 inches, ca. 1950s. $10-15.

New Mexico plate, Land of Enchantment New Mexico, 8 inches, ca. 1960s. *Courtesy of Gertrude Templeton Sasser and Otis C. Sasser.* $8-12.

New Mexico plate, Carlsbad Caverns, 10 inches, ca. 1960s. *Courtesy of Shirley Falardeau.* $8-12.

New Mexico plate, Made in Japan, 7.5 inches, ca. 1960s. *Courtesy of Old Mill Antiques.* $4-8.

New Mexico plate, Vernon Kilns, Carlsbad Caverns, New Mexico, 10.25 inches, ca. 1950s. *Courtesy of Old Mill Antiques.* $25-35.

New Mexico plate, 9.25 inches, ca. 1940s. $4-8.

New Mexico plate, Sabin Crest-O-Gold, Souvenir of New Mexico, 7.25 inches, ca. 1940s. $12-18.

New Mexico, Vernon Kilns, Picture Map Plate of New Mexico, 10.5 inches, ca. 1940s. *Courtesy of Out 'n' Back Antiques.* $25-35.

New Mexico plate, 9 inches, ca. 1960s. *Courtesy of Mr. and Mrs. Earl Cox.* $8-12.

New Mexico plate, Vernon Kilns, 10.5 inches, ca. 1940s. *Courtesy of Out 'n' Back Antiques.* $25-35.

New York

New York City plate, ca. 1950s. *Courtesy of Mr. and Mrs. Earl Cox*. $10-15.

New York plate, The Empire State, 9 inches, ca. 1950s. *Courtesy of Mr. and Mrs. Earl Cox*. $4-8.

New York plate, National Association of Postmasters of the United States commemorative, 8.5 inches, ca. 1990. $12-18.

New York plate, Buffalo: My Kind of Town, 9 inches, ca. 1980s. *Courtesy of Gertrude Templeton Sasser and Otis C. Sasser.* $5-10.

New York plate, Niagara Falls Prospect Point plate, 8 inches, ca. 1950s. *Courtesy of Gertrude Templeton Sasser and Otis C. Sasser.* $5-10.

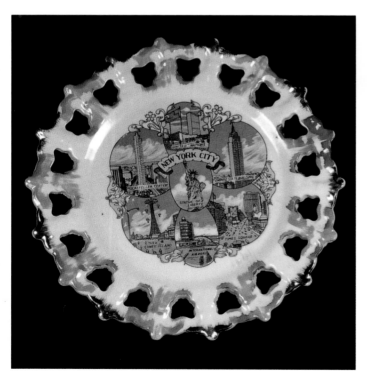

New York plate, Japan, New York City, 8 inches, ca. 1960s. *Courtesy of Gertrude Templeton Sasser and Otis C. Sasser.* $5-10.

New York plate, decorated by Delano Studios, Sagamore Hill, Oyster Bay, Long Island, New York, 10 inches, ca. 1970s. $25-35.

New York plate, Vernon Kilns, Statue of Liberty, 10.5 inches, ca. 1940s. *Courtesy of Out 'n' Back Antiques.* $25-35.

New York plate, decorated by ENCO, Views of America Series, Empire State Bldg., New York City, 9 inches, ca. 1950s. $20-25.

North Carolina

North Carolina plate, The Tar Heel State, 9 inches, ca. 1960s. $12-18.

North Carolina plate, The Tar Heel State, 9.25 inches, ca. 1960s.
Courtesy of Gertrude Templeton Sasser and Otis C. Sasser. $12-18.

North Carolina plate, Colonial China, 7.5 x 7.5 inches ca. 1950s.
Courtesy of Gertrude Templeton Sasser and Otis C. Sasser. $15-22.

North Carolina plate, Tweetsie Railroad Blowing Rock, N.C., ca.
1950s. *Courtesy of Out 'n' Back Antiques.* $15-20.

North Dakota

North Dakota plate, Homer Laughlin, Breadbasket of the World, 9 inches, ca. 1950s. *Courtesy of Kenneth L. Surratt, Jr.* $18-22.

North Dakota plate, Breadbasket of the World, 9 inches, ca. 1950s. $4-8.

Ohio

Ohio plate, Sabin, 9.25 inches, ca. 1960s. $18-22.

Ohio plate, Sheffield, U. S. A., 10.5 inches, ca. 1960s. *Courtesy of JoAnn Askew.* $16-25.

Ohio plate, Sabin, The Buckeye State, 9 inches, ca. 1960s. *Courtesy of Margie Manning.* $12-18.

Ohio plate, Dayton, Ohio, Birthplace of Aviation, 7.25 inches, ca. 1950s. *Courtesy of Jackie McDonald.* $5-10.

Ohio plate, Mother of Presidents, ca. 1960s. *Courtesy of Mary G. Moon.* $5-10.

Ohio plate, The Buckeye State, 9.25 inches, ca. 1960s. *Courtesy of JoAnn Askew.* $4-8.

Ohio plate, The Buckeye State, 9 inches, ca. 1960s. *Courtesy of Mr. and Mrs. Earl Cox.* $4-8.

Oklahoma

Oklahoma plate, 7 inches, ca. 1960s. *Courtesy of Mary G. Moon.* $5-10.

Oklahoma plate, Oklahoma City, 6 inches, ca. 1970s. $4-8.

Oklahoma plate, The Sooner State, 9.5 inches, ca. 1960s. *Courtesy of Gertrude Templeton Sasser and Otis C. Sasser.* $8-12.

Oklahoma plate, The Sooner State, 9 inches, ca. 1960s. $4-8.

Oklahoma plate, The Sooner State, 7.25 inches, ca. 1960s. *Courtesy of Margaret McRaney.* $4-8.

Oklahoma plate, Sabin, The Sooner State, ca. 1960s. *Courtesy of Mary G. Moon.* $12-15.

Oklahoma plate, 8 inches, ca. 1960s. *Courtesy of Mr. and Mrs. Earl Cox.* $4-8.

Oregon

Oregon plate, Made in Japan, Oregon Pacific Wonderland, 8 inches, ca. 1960s. *Courtesy of Mary G. Moon.* $4-8.

Oregon plate, 9.25 inches, ca. 1960s. *Courtesy of Mr. and Mrs. Earl Cox.* $4-8.

Oregon plate, Centennial 1859-1959, 8 inches. $6-12.

Oregon plate, 7 inches, ca. 1960s. *Courtesy of Gertrude Templeton Sasser and Otis C. Sasser.* $4-8.

Oregon plate, Pacific Wonderland, 5.5 inches, ca. 1960s. $2-4.

Portland, Vernon Kilns, Oregon plate, 10.5 inches, ca. 1940s. *Courtesy of Out 'n' Back Antiques.* $25-35.

Pennsylvania

Pennsylvania plate, Kettlesprings Kilns, New Bethlehem Pennsylvania Centennial commemorative 1853-1953, 9.75 inches. *Courtesy of Kenneth L. Surratt, Jr.* $12-18.

Pennsylvania plate, Valley Forge, Pa., The Memorial Bell Tower, 10.25 inches, 1952. *Courtesy of Memory Lane Mall.* $20-35.

Pennsylvania plate, Indian Museum Near Brookville, Pa., 9.5 inches, ca. 1960s. $10-15.

Pennsylvania plate, The Amish Country plate, 7.25 inches, ca. 1980s. $5-10.

Pennsylvania plate, Philadelphia, City of Brotherly Love, 7.25 inches, ca. 1950s. *Courtesy of Old Mill Antiques.* $10-15.

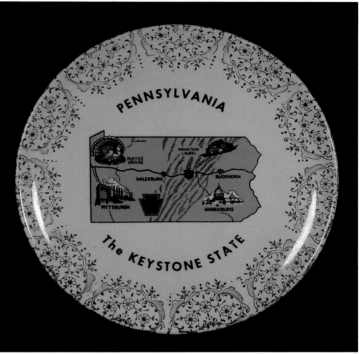

Pennsylvania plate, The Keystone State, 9 inches, ca. 1960s. *Courtesy of Mr. and Mrs. Earl Cox.* $4-8.

Pennsylvania plate, Keystone State, 9.25 inches, ca. 1960s. *Courtesy of JoAnn Askew.* $4-8.

Pennsylvania plate, Poconos, Rose China, Grecian Princess, 6.75 inches, ca. 1950s. $10-15.

Pennsylvania plate, Heart of the Amish Country, 9.25 inches, ca. 1970s. $8-12.

Pennsylvania plate, Bicentennial Philadelphia 1776-1976, Liberty Bell, 6.25 inches. $4-8.

Pennsylvania plate, Winona Five Falls, Bushkill, 7.25 inches, ca. 1980s. $8-12.

Pennsylvania plate, Vernon Kilns, 10.5 inches, ca. 1940s. *Courtesy of Antiques Out 'n' Back*. $35-45.

Pennsylvania plate, Gettysburg, Pa. 1863, Eternal Light Peace Memorial, 9 inches, ca. 1950s. $18-22.

Rhode Island

Rhode Island plate, "Little Rhody," 8 inches, ca. 1960s. *Courtesy of Gertrude Templeton Sasser and Otis C. Sasser.* $4-8.

Rhode Island plate, 9 inches, ca. 1960s. *Courtesy of Mr. and Mrs. Earl Cox.* $4-8.

South Carolina

South Carolina plate, South Carolina The Palmetto State, 9 inches, ca. 1960s. $4-8.

South Carolina plate, The Palmetto State, 9 inches, ca. 1960s. *Courtesy of Gertrude Templeton Sasser and Otis C. Sasser*. $4-8.

South Carolina plate, 9 inches, ca. 1980s. $6-12.

South Carolina plate, Vernon Kilns, Sumter South Carolina, 10.5 inches, ca. 1940s. *Courtesy of Out 'n' Back Antiques*. $25-35.

South Carolina plate, 9.25 inches, ca. 1960s. $8-12.

South Dakota

South Dakota plate, Mt. Rushmore National Memorial, Black Hills, 10.5 inches, ca. 1960s. $18-25.

South Dakota plate, Black Hills, 7 inches, ca. 1960s. $5-10.

South Dakota plate, Made in Japan, Black Hills and Badlands, 4 inches, ca. 1980s. $3-6.

South Dakota plate, Scenic South Dakota, 9.25 inches, ca. 1960s. $10-15.

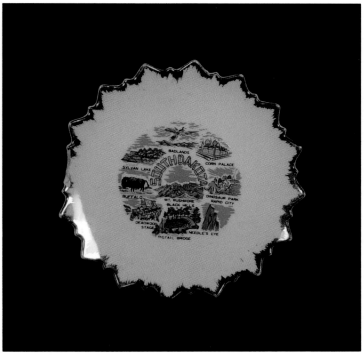

South Dakota plate, 7 inches, ca. 1960s. *Courtesy of Mr. and Mrs. Earl Cox.* $4-8.

South Dakota plate, Made in Korea, Black Hills So. Dak., 7 inches, ca. 1970s. *Courtesy of Old Mill Antiques.* $4-8.

Tennessee

Tennessee plate, Opryland USA, 10 inches, ca. 1970s. $10-15.

Tennessee plate, 9.5 inches, ca. 1960s. *Courtesy of Gertrude Templeton Sasser and Otis C. Sasser.* $8-12.

Tennessee plate, Homer Laughlin, Cavalier, Eggshell, 10.25 inches, ca. 1940s. *Courtesy of Old Mill Antiques.* $12-18.

Tennessee plate, Homer Laughlin, Cavalier, Eggshell, 9.25 inches, ca. 1940s. *Courtesy of Jackie McDonald.* $8-12.

Tennessee plate, Memphis Tenn., 9.25 inches, ca. 1960s. *Courtesy of JoAnn Askew*. $4-8.

Tennessee plate, Made in Korea, 8 inches, ca. 1970s. $4-8.

Tennessee plate, Gatlinburg, Tenn., Foot of the Great Smoky Mts., 9 inches, ca. 1970s. *Courtesy of Louise Martin*. $10-15.

Tennessee plate, Made in Korea, 8 inches, ca. 1970s. $4-8.

Tennessee plate, Made in Japan, Rock City, 5 inches, ca. 1960s. *Courtesy of Old Mill Antiques*. $4-8.

Tennessee plate, 8 inches, ca. 1970s. *Courtesy of Gertrude Templeton Sasser and Otis C. Sasser*. $4-8.

Tennessee plate, Made in Korea, Nashville, 7.5 inches, ca. 1970s. *Courtesy of Gertrude Templeton Sasser and Otis C. Sasser*. $4-8.

Tennessee plate, Made in Japan, Nashville, Tenn., 8 inches, ca. 1970s. $4-8.

Tennessee plate, Opryland USA, Home of American Music, 10 inches, ca. 1960s. $10-15.

Tennessee plate, The Volunteer State, 7 inches, ca. 1970s. *Courtesy of Mr. and Mrs. Earl Cox.* $4-8.

Tennessee plate, Memphis, Tenn., Home of the Cotton Carnival, 9 inches, ca. 1960s. *Courtesy of Gertrude Templeton Sasser and Otis C. Sasser.* $10-15.

Tennessee plate, Vernon Kilns, Oak Ridge, Tennessee, ca. 10.5 inches, ca. 1940s. *Courtesy of Out 'n' Back Antiques.* $25-35.

Tennessee plate, Vernon Kilns, Chattanooga, Tennessee, 10.5 inches, ca. 1940s. *Courtesy of Out 'n' Back Antiques.* $35-45.

Texas

Texas plate, Texarkana Arkansas and Texas Centennial, 10 inches, ca. 1973. *Courtesy of Jackie McDonald.* $5-10.

Texas plate, Longview Centennial, 10 inches, ca. 1970. *Courtesy of Margie Manning.* $5-10

Texas plate, Limited Edition, A Living Page of Texas History commemorating Sesquicentennial, Jefferson, Texas, 9 inches, 1986. *Courtesy of Gold Leaf Antique Mall.* $10-15.

Texas plate, signed Made in U. S. A., Astroworld, 8 inches, ca. 1970s. *Courtesy of Gertrude Templeton Sasser and Otis C. Sasser.* $8-12.

Texas plate, Presidential, 10 inches, ca. 1960s.
Courtesy of Gertrude Templeton Sasser and Otis C. Sasser. $22-30.

Texas plate, Big Bend National Park, 9.75 inches, ca. 1960s. $12-18.

Texas plate, Pioneer Town 7-A Ranch Resort, Wimberly, 7.25 inches, ca. 1980s.
Courtesy of Old Mill Antiques. $10-15.

Texas plate, Ettie R. Garner Building plate, Uvalde, Texas, 10 inches, ca. 1950s. *Courtesy of Jackie McDonald.* $4-8.

Texas plate, Official Commemorative Limited Edition Texas Sesquicentennial, The Lone Star State, 10 inches, 1986. *Courtesy of Gertrude Templeton Sasser and Otis C. Sasser.* $12-18.

Texas plate, Sabin, Port Isabel, Texas, 9.25 inches, ca. 1960s. $4-8.

Texas plate, Dallas Texas, 9 inches, ca. 1950s. *Courtesy of Gertrude Templeton Sasser and Otis C. Sasser.* $8-12.

Texas plate, Made in Japan, Big Tex, ca. 1960s. *Courtesy of Mary G. Moon.* $4-8.

Texas plate, Souvenir of the Lone Star State, 6 inches, ca. 1960s. *Courtesy of Memory Lane Mall.* $4-8.

Texas plate, Houston, 7.5 inches, ca. 1950s. *Courtesy of Mary G. Moon.* $3-7.

Texas plate, Lone Star State, 7 inches, ca. 1960s. *Courtesy of Mr. and Mrs. Earl Cox.* $4-8.

Texas plate, 7.5 inches, ca. 1960s. *Courtesy of Gertrude Templeton Sasser and Otis C. Sasser.* $4-8.

Texas plate, The Alamo, 8 inches, ca. 1960s. *Courtesy of Gertrude Templeton Sasser and Otis C. Sasser.* $5-10.

Texas plate, Kettlesprings Kilns, Fort Bend County Sesquicentennial, 1822 to 1972, 9.5 inches. *Courtesy of Gertrude Templeton Sasser and Otis C. Sasser.* $12-18.

Texas plate, Six Flags Over Texas, 9.5 inches, ca. 1970s. *Courtesy of JoAnn Askew.* $10-15.

Texas plate, Dallas, 10.5 inches, ca. 1950s. *Courtesy of JoAnn Askew.* $12-18.

Texas plate, Tower of the America's, World's Fair in San Antonio, 4 inches, 1968. $4-8.

Texas plate, San Antonio Hemisfair, 1968 World's Fair, 7 inches. $12-18.

Texas plate, Made in Japan, World's Fair in San Antonio, 6 inches, 1968. *Courtesy of Old Mill Antiques.*$10-15.

Texas plate, The Lone Star State, 10 inches, ca. 1940s. *Courtesy of Old Mill Antiques.* $12-18.

Texas Plate, Staffordshire Royal Winton, San Antonio, 9.5 inches, 1951. *Courtesy of Old Mill Antiques.* $45-65.

Texas plate, San Antonio Texas, 8.5 inches, ca. 1960s. $4-8.

Texas plate, Homer Laughlin, Padre Island National Seashore, Corpus Christi, 9 inches, ca. 1960s. $8-12.

Texas plate, Homer Laughlin, Inner Space, 9 inches, ca. 1960s. $8-12.

Texas plate, 10 inches, ca. 1960s. *Courtesy of Louise Martin.* $10-15.

Texas plate, The Lone Star State, 7.25 inches, ca. 1960s. *Courtesy of Gold Leaf Antique Mall.* $12-18.

Texas plate, The Lone Star State, 9.25 inches, ca. 1960s. *Courtesy of Gold Leaf Antique Mall.* $4-8.

Texas plate, Corpus Christi, 9 inches, ca. 1960s. $4-8.

Texas plate, Corpus Christi, ca. 1960s. *Courtesy of Out 'n' Back Antiques.* $12-15.

Texas plate, Vernon Kilns, Bandera Centennial 1853-1953, 10.5 inches. *Courtesy of Out 'n' Back Antiques.* $25-35.

Texas plate, Vernon Kilns, Fort Worth Centennial 1849-1949, 10.5 inches. *Courtesy of Out 'n' Back Antiques.* $25-35.

Utah

Utah plate, Land of Color, 9.5 inches, ca. 1960s. *Courtesy of Gertrude Templeton Sasser and Otis C. Sasser.* $12-18.

Utah plate, green and gold border, 10 inches, ca. 1940s. $18-22.

Utah plate, Salt Lake City, 10 inches, ca. 1940s. *Courtesy of Old Mill Antiques.* $18-22.

Utah plate, Homer Laughlin, 9 inches, ca. 1960s. *Courtesy of Kenneth L. Surratt, Jr.* $12-18.

Utah plate, ca. 1960s. *Courtesy of Mary G. Moon.* $12-18.

Utah plate, Made in Japan, 10.25 inches, ca. 1960s. *Courtesy of Old Mill Antiques.* $15-20.

Vermont

Vermont plate, ca. 1950s, 9 inches. $4-8.

Vermont plate, ca. 1950s. *Courtesy of Out 'n' Back Antiques.* $10-15.

Vermont plate, Vernon Kiln, This is Vermont, Green Mountain State, 10.5 inches, ca. 1940s. *Courtesy of Out 'n' Back Antiques.* $25-35.

Vermont plate, 8 inches, ca. 1950s. *Courtesy of Out 'n' Back Antiques.* $10-15.

Virginia

Virginia plate, Vernon Kilns, Famous Shrines in Historical Virginia, 10 inches, ca. 1950s. *Courtesy of Memory Lane Mall.* $25-35.

Virginia plate, Wedgwood, The Capitol, Williamsburg, 9 inches, 1953. $45-65.

Virginia plate, The Common Glory, Williamsburg, Va., 9.75 inches, ca. 1950s. *Courtesy of Memory Lane Mall.* $12-18.

Virginia plate, Williamsburg, Virginia, 7 inches, ca. 1950s. *Courtesy of Ollie Clements.* $5-10.

Virginia plate, State Capitol, 9 inches, ca. 1960s. *Courtesy of Old Mill Antiques.* $22-28.

Virginia plate, 7.5 inches, ca. 1960s. *Courtesy of Gertrude Templeton Sasser and Otis C. Sasser.* $6-12.

Virginia plate, Mother of Presidents, 6 inches, ca. 1970s. $12-18.

Virginia plate, DeLano Studios, Mount Vernon hand colored, 10 inches, ca. 1950s. *Courtesy of Ollie Clements.* $22-28.

Virginia plate, Mother of Presidents, ca. 1940s. *Courtesy of Mr. and Mrs. Earl Cox.* $4-8.

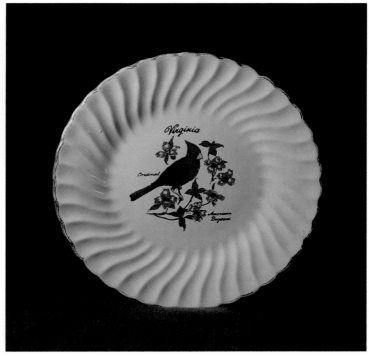

Virginia plate, 7.25 inches, ca. 1970s. $10-15.

Virginia plate, Shenandoah Natl. Park Skyline Drive, 4.5 inches, ca. 1960s. $5-10.

Virginia plate, decorated by Delano Studios, Governor's Palace Williamsburg, 10 inches, ca. 1960s. $22-28.

Virginia plate, Williamsburg, Governor's Palace, 10 inches, ca. 1970s. $35-45.

Virginia plate, decorated by Delano Studios, Raleigh Tavern Williamsburg, 10 inches, ca. 1960s. $22-28.

Virginia plate, Vernon Kilns, Portsmouth Bicentennial 1752-1952, 10.5 inches. *Courtesy of Out 'n'
Back Antiques.* $25-35.

Back of Portsmouth plate.

Virginia plate, Vernon Kilns, 10.5
inches, ca. 1950s. *Courtesy of Out 'n'
Back Antiques.* $35-45.

Washington

Washington State plate, Made in Japan, scenes from the state, 7 x 6.75 inches, ca. 1960s. $4-8.

Washington State plate, 8.5 inches, ca. 1940s. $22-28.

Washington State plate, Made in Japan, Space Needle, 9 inches, ca. 1960s. $4-8.

Washington State plate, ca. 1940s. *Courtesy of Mr. and Mrs. Earl Cox.* $4-8.

West Virginia

West Virginia plate, 8.25 x 8.25 inches, ca. 1960s. $18-22.

West Virginia plate, State Capitol, Charleston, W. Va., 9.25 inches, ca. 1950s. $12-18.

West Virginia plate, 9 inches, ca. 1950s.
Courtesy of Mr. and Mrs. Earl Cox. $4-8.

Wisconsin

Wisconsin plate, The Badger State, 9 inches, ca. 1960s. $4-8.

Wisconsin plate, Homer Laughlin, Wascott, Wis., 9 inches, ca. 1960s. $8-12.

Wisconsin plate, The Badger State, 9 inches, ca. 1960s. $4-8.

Wisconsin plate, 8.5 inches, ca. 1950s. *Courtesy of Mr. and Mrs. Earl Cox.* $12-18.

Wyoming

Wyoming, Homer Laughlin, Yellowstone, 10.25 inches, ca. 1940s. $12-18.

Wyoming, Yellowstone Park, 10.25 inches, ca. 1960s. *Courtesy of Old Mill Antiques*. $5-10.

Wyoming, Made in Japan, Old Faithful Yellowstone, 6 inches, ca. 1950s. $5-10.

Wyoming plate, Made in Korea, Wonderful Wyoming, 7 inches, ca. 1980s. *Courtesy of Old Mill Antiques*. $8-12.

Wyoming plate, gold border, 6 inches, ca. 1950s. *Courtesy of Mr. and Mrs. Earl Cox*. $15-20.

Wyoming plate, Little America Wyoming, 9.5 inches, ca. 1950s. $12-18.

Wyoming plate, Wonderful Wyoming, 7.25 inches, ca. 1950s. $4-8.

Wyoming plate, Vernon Kilns, 10.5 inches, ca. 1950s. *Courtesy of Out 'n' Back Antiques.* $35-45.

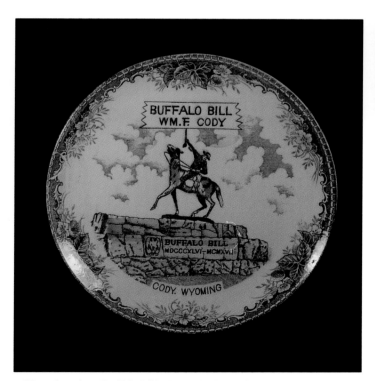

Wyoming plate, Buffalo Bill Wm. F. Cody, Cody, Wyoming, ca. 1940s. *Courtesy of Out 'n' Back Antiques.* $15-20.

FIRST METHODIST CHURCH
CROWLEY, LA.

Chapter Three

Church Plates

Arkansas

Belleville United Methodist Church, Belleville, Arkansas, plate, 10 inches, ca. 1950s. $10-15.

Decorated by World Wide Art Studios, Sylvania Presbyterian Church, Ward, Arkansas, plate, 9 inches, ca. 1950s. $12-18.

California

Back of plate with Homer Laughlin mark and World Wide Art Studio mark.

Homer Laughlin Theme pattern and decorated by World Wide Art Studios Liberty Baptist Church and Community House plate, Los Angeles, California, ca. 1940. *Courtesy of Mary G. Moon*. $15-20.

Back of First Mission Baptist Church plate.

Decorated by World Wide Studios, First Mission Baptist Church plate, Santa Ana, California, ca. 1950s. *Courtesy of Mary G. Moon*. $10-15.

Louisiana

Decorated by World Wide Art Studios, First Methodist Church plate, Crowley, Louisiana, ca. 1950s. *Courtesy of Mary G. Moon.* $10-15.

New York

Adam Antique by Steubenville, Cathedral of St. John the Divine plate, New York City, 10 inches, ca. 1940s. *Courtesy of JoAnn Askew.* $20-30.

Hand painted by Delano Studios, First Presbyterian Church plate, Babylon, Long Island, New York 1730-1980, 10.75 inches. $15-20.

Pennsylvania

Homer Laughlin Eggshell Theme plate decorated by World Wide Art Studios, Missionary Baptist Church plate, Corsicana, Texas, 9.5 inches, 1940. $20-25.

Fifth Avenue Methodist Church plate, New Brighton, Pennsylvania, 8 inches, ca. 1960s. *Courtesy of Old Mill Antiques*. $10-15.

Decorated by World Wide Art Studios, First Baptist Church plate, Grapevine, Texas 1854-1954, 9.5 inches. $15-20.

Homer Laughlin Eggshell Theme plate decorated by World Wide Art Studios, St. Matthews United Methodist Church plate, Houston, Texas, ca. 1940. *Courtesy of Gertrude Templeton Sasser and Otis C. Sasser.* $20-30.

Epworth United Methodist Church plate, Houston, Texas, 10 inches, ca. 1960s. *Courtesy of Margie Manning.* $10-15.

Back of Bethesda Baptist Church plate with World Wide Art Studios mark.

Decorated by World Wide Art Studios, Bethesda Baptist Church plate, Marshall, Texas, ca. 1950s. *Courtesy of Mary G. Moon.* $15-20.

Decorated by World Wide Art Studios, Maud Methodist Church plate, Maud, Texas, 10 inches, ca. 1950s. *Courtesy of JoAnn Askew.* $15-20.

Homer Laughlin Eggshell Theme plate decorated by World Wide Art Studios, McLean Methodist Church, McLean, Texas, 9.5 inches, ca. 1940. $20-25.

Homer Laughlin Eggshell Theme, Tapp Memorial Methodist Church plate, New Boston, Texas, 10 inches, ca. 1940s. $25-30.

Homer Laughlin Eggshell Theme, First Methodist Church plate, Sulphur Springs, Texas, 10 inches, ca. 1940. $25-30.

Decorated by World Wide Art Studios, Highland Park Baptist Church plate, Texarkana, Texas, 10 inches, ca. 1960s. *Courtesy of JoAnn Askew.* $25-30.

Back of Hopewell C.M.E. Temple plate showing the Homer Laughlin Eggshell Georgian mark and the World Wide Art Studios mark.

Homer Laughlin Eggshell Georgian plate decorated by World Wide Art Studios, Hopewell C.M.E. Temple, Texarkana, Texas, 1931. *Courtesy of Mary G. Moon.* $25-35.

Chapter Four

Foreign Plates and Related Items

Made in Western Germany, Quebec, Canada plate, ca. 1940s. *Courtesy of Mary G. Moon.* $25-35.

Masons, Souvenir of Niagara Falls plate, Canada, 9 inches, ca. 1940s. $25-35.

Butchart Gardens trivet, Victoria B.C. Canada, 6 inches, ca. 1960s. *Courtesy of Mary G. Moon.* $12-15.

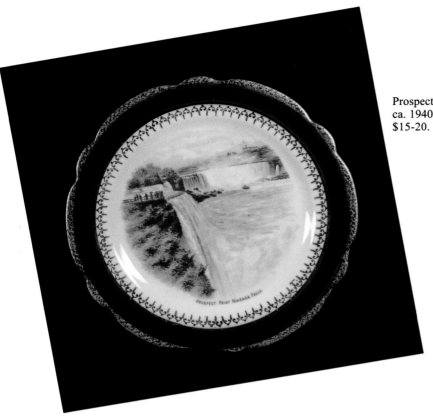

Prospect Point Niagara Falls plate, 6.5 inches, ca. 1940s. *Courtesy of Jackie McDonald.* $15-20.

Made in Germany, Church, Harvey, N.B., 5.75 inches, ca. 1930s. *Courtesy of Gold Leaf Antique Mall.* $15-20.

Handpainted Canada plate, ca. 1950s. $15-20.

Royal Winton, Canada plate, 9.5 inches, ca. 1960s. *Courtesy of Gertrude Templeton Sasser and Otis C. Sasser.* $15-20.

Canadian Mountie plate, 6 inches, ca. 1950s. *Courtesy of Margie Manning.* $15-20.

Made in Japan, Canada Coats-of-Arms & Emblems plate, 10 inches, ca. 1950s. $10-15.

Queens University, Kingston, Ontario ashtray, 3.62 inches, ca. 1950s. $8-12.

Alberta plate, 12 inches, ca. 1960s. $15-18.

Japan, Windsor Canada ashtray, 3.5 inches, ca. 1950s. $5-8.

Collingswoods Bone China England, Alberta, Canada Bridge & South Saskatchewan River, Medicine Hat plate, 9.25 inches x 8.75 inches, ca. 1930s. $20-25.

Stamped Made in Japan, Royal Canadian Mounted Police dish, 5 inches, ca. 1950s. $5-10.

Candis-Canada, Coat of Arms of Canada plate, 9.5 inches, ca. 1960s. $9-12.

Crown Devon Fieldings, Court House, Estevan, Saskatchewan, Canada ashtray, 4.75 x 4.75 inches, ca. 1940s. $12-18.

Made in Japan, Souvenir of Canada Niagara Falls plate, Canada, 7 inches, ca. 1950s. $10-12.

Virgin Islands plate with iridescent border, 10 inches, ca. 1970s. *Courtesy of Memory Lane Mall*. $9-12.

Isn't it great to be in the Virgin Islands ashtray, 6 inches x 6 inches, ca. 1960s. $7-9.

Nassau Bahamas Island of New Providence plate, 10 inches, ca. 1980s. *Courtesy of Gertrude Templeton Sasser and Otis C. Sasser*. $10-12.

The Bahama Islands plate, ca. 1980s. $10-12.

Bermuda Islands plate, 8.25 inches, ca. 1960s. $12-15.

Puerto Rico plate, 10.5 inches, ca. 1980s. *Courtesy of JoAnn Askew.* $10-12.

St. Thomas Virgin Islands plate, 9 inches, ca. 1960s. $12-15.

Grindley England, Salisbury Cathedral plate, 9.25 inches, ca. 1950s. *Courtesy of Mary G. Moon.* $20-25.

Hand painted Stavangerflint Oslo plate, 7 x 7 inches, ca. 1960s. *Courtesy of Shirley Faldareau.* $35-45.

Piccadilly Circus plate mark.

A.J. Wilkinson Ltd. Burdem, England Piccadilly Circus
plate, 9 inches x 9 inches, ca. 1960s. $35-45.

Bavaria porcelain Der Rhein plate, 10
inches, ca. 1950s. $25-35.

Alt Osterreich ashtray, 5 inches x 4.75 inches, ca. 1960s. $12-15.

Germany plate signed "Melilla" depicting Frankfurt/Main, 7.5 inches, ca. 1960s. $12-15.

Bavaria Market Remlingen plate, 7.75 inches, ca. 1950s. $15-18.

Salzburg Ashtray, 4.75 inches, ca. 1950s. $8-12.

Arklow Made in Republic of Ireland, ashtray, 4.75 inches, ca. 1960s. $12-15.

Signed Hutschenreuther Germany Souvenir Roma plate, 7.5 inches, ca. 1950s. $25-35.

Bavaria Schonding, Roma-Basilica di St. Pietro, 8,25 inches, ca. 1940s. $25-35.

Bavaria, Frankfurt a.M. ashtray, 5 inches, ca. 1950s. *Courtesy of Mary G. Moon.* $12-15.

NCO-EM Wives Club plate, 9.5 inches, ca. 1960s. *Courtesy of Memory Lane Mall.* $15-20.

West German Berlin vase, 4.5 inches,
ca. 1950s. *Courtesy of Mary G. Moon.*
$15-20.

Bavarian Gruss aus Kircheimbolanden ashtray,
3.75 inches, ca. 1950s. $12-15.

Jerusalem plate, 5 inches, ca. 1970s. $12-15.

London plate, Weatherby Henley England Falcon Ware, 7 inches, ca. 1950s. *Courtesy of Out 'n' Back Antiques*. $10-15.

Central District Hong Kong 1983. *Courtesy of Out 'n' Back Antiques*. $10-15.

Central District Hong Kong 1860, ca. 1980s. *Courtesy of Out 'n' Back Antiques*. $10-15.

Thomas Beauchamp Earl of Warwick plate, made in England, 8 inches, ca. 1950s. $15-20.

Souvenir De Paris ashtray, Limoges, ca. 1960s. $15-25.

Bibliography

Altman, Seymour and Violet. *The Book of Buffalo Pottery*. Atglen, Pennsylvania: Schiffer Publishing Ltd., 1997.

Burgess, Arene Wiemers. *Collector's Guide to Souvenir Plates*. Atglen, Pennsylvania: Schiffer Publishing Ltd., 1996.

Cunningham, Jo. *The Collector's Encyclopedia of American Dinnerware*. Paducah, Kentucky: Collector Books, 1982.

Jasper, Joanne. *The Collector's Encyclopedia of Homer Laughlin China Reference & Value Guide*. Paducah, Kentucky: Collector Books, 1993.

Kovel, Ralph & Terry. *Kovels' New Dictionary of Marks*. New York: Crown Publishers, Inc., 1986.

Lehner, Lois. *Lehner's Encyclopedia of U.S. Marks on Pottery, Porcelain & Clay*. Paducah, Kentucky: Collector's Books, 1988.

Nelson, Maxine Feek. *Collectible Vernon Kilns: An Identification and Value Guide*. Paducah, Kentucky: Collector Books, 1994.

Snyder, Jeffrey B. *Historical Staffordshire: American Patriots & Views*. Atglen, Pennsylvania: Schiffer Publishing Ltd., 1995.

Watson, Howard and Pat. *The Clarice Cliff Colour Price Guide*. London: Francis Joseph Publications, 1995.